THE NIGHT
KNOWS
YOUR NAME

The Night Knows Your Name

ISBN: 978-0-6488016-1-0

Front cover image and

Book design by *Dvora Dali*

First printing edition March 2020

Second printing edition November 2020

Table of Contents

Eivør Dali

Acknowledgements

I would like to thank the miracle of who I call my *art god* Salvador Dali, who would not have created a lot of the work he did without his wife and muse Gala, who I also offer much of my gratitude to. Further thanks must go to, Carl Jung and his work on the integration of the shadow self; Baba Ram Dass, Alan Watts, Rumi and Lao Tzu for their spiritual teachings; Russell Brand and his infinitely generous videos and podcasts; Jordan Peterson for the lectures and interviews posted online that led me to my fascination with Jung; Marcus Aurelius and Epictetus for their contributions to stoicism; alongside the teachings of Buddhist practice and mindfulness; and the books: "Siddhartha" by Herman Hesse, and "The Prophet" by Khalil Gibran.

I would also like to thank the musicians that moved me through the writing of a lot of the poems you will read in this book: Sevdaliza, FKA Twigs, Heilung, Eivør, Wardruna, Aurora, Jeff Buckley, Incubus, Tom

The Night Knows Your Name

Waits, SYML, Massive Attack, Rosalia, Muse, Queens of the Stone Age, Audioslave, Radiohead, Slipknot, to name a few of the key players. Alongside the musicians, the writers, art directors for the world of Penny Dreadful, Hannibal Lecter, Game of Thrones and the Lord of the Rings that fed my appetite for the fantastical, macabre, light and dark that has evidently created the hunger in me to create my own kind of mystical world.

Apart from these familiar names, a few that are not so familiar but need to be known: First of all, I'd like to thank the poetry community on Instagram, without whom I would have not gained the confidence to pursue publishing this book. In particular, new formed friendships through this community who have brought me through some tough moments. Also, the ones who have been supporting me from my awkward first week of posting, I see you, and your support means the world to me.

Next, I'd like to thank my psychologist, Dr. Chew, for her knowledge, understanding and empathy towards my trauma and recovery, and the dedication she continues to have, laughing with me through my confusion, cheering me on with every little breakthrough, every step of the way.

No less, I'd like to thank my parents for encouraging me to draw, write, and play music when I was little; for doing their best, and loving me in the way they knew.

Lastly, but never the least, my heart and muse, Tahir, who I have been separated from for so long, but remains the closest to me. My gratitude

Avora Dali

to him cannot be summarised in a small amount of words, but he is the one who continues to keep my heart warm, and young. I am better through the gentleness, adventure, faith, hope and home I share with him. For his patience, forgiveness, wisdom, loyalty, insight, creativity, and quick wit have given me friendship when I thought I was alone, wisdom when I had none, and love when I didn't deserve it; Without whom, I would have struggled to write this book. He has humbled me, and taught me how to love.

Thank you for everything.

Preface

I want to help end the stigma of mental health and illuminate the silver lining for those who struggle to step forward. I was always a very creative person but I have previously always been ashamed to express myself, thinking that part of me should only be reserved for the people in my heart, in private setting; who would endearingly exclaim, "you're a gypsy!" "You're a musician!" "You're an artist!" and although I so badly wanted to be any of the above, I never believed it was an option for me., until I was forced into doing something to keep me busy when I began therapy in 2018, after having quit another job. This made me realise that I'd been trying too hard to achieve a certain kind of normalcy that I was perhaps unable to, or never meant to achieve in the first place.

Thus, the birth of my artistry, more specifically, my writing career (which looked like an awkwardly formatted poem on social media); although I would have never called it a plausible career back then, nor would I have thought I could possibly turn it into a career. If you ask me today, I always wanted to be an artist (secretly) and still do. I feel like I'm slowly coming out of that closet — and there's a lot of skeletons in there, so you can imagine, it works out in a lot of ways.

Life was difficult with undiagnosed mental illness. I quit jobs, failed at relationships, friendships, moved homes too many times, started things and never finished them. Although, through my ignorance, I developed a very close relationship with, and insatiable appetite for: knowing the truth, discovering my place in the world, learning about who I am, and possibly finding some semblance of peace (through philosophy, psychology and spirituality, which you will find heavily soaking the pages of this book).

Truer things will always remain true regardless, but if you ask me to give you the answers in the next line, I won't — I believe everyone needs to go through their own journey to break out of their shells and learn to love, and water the person they really are to become the person they really want to be. Instead, I hope I can help point you in the right direction, or help you find the courage to create the life you've always wanted for yourself. May this book serve as inspiration, and the catalyst for that journey within yourself.

We are often afraid of the things we cannot see — but I am here to take you on my personal journey of seeing my unseen. The Night Knows Your Name is a collection of poetry I started writing in conjunction with my therapy. It served as a great means of externalising and exploring the themes of heartbreak, despair, anger, confusion through my early days of recovery. I was also able to relive my joy, and cement little pieces of wisdom I discovered along the way. These pieces inevitably paved a clearer road for my journey inward to clearer sight of who I really am, which has now led me to you.

I expected linear progression of darkness to light for my healing, but it hasn't been the case at all. In my despair, there were moments of joy and revelation. In revelation, there were bleak moments of despair. I have sectioned the book according to emotional themes: Ghost Love, Sorrow, Anguish, Healing, Way, Fire, and Home - and you can read it in that order as a journey to the light, or pick a poem from a chapter that your heart yearns to read from; some can serve as prayers, which you can recite as mantras, which you can meditate upon whenever you are idle. Wherever you are on your journey, I hope you honour it, and whichever way you choose to read this book, I hope you will begin to learn your name in the night, just as I have begun to learn mine.

This second printing edition has been reformatted with chapter labels, and slight amendments to the acknowledgements and author biography, an updated contact page, and a complete cover redesign.

Diora Dali

My dearest Tahir

You have made me better

آپ کے لئے میری محبت کو الفاظ بیان نہیں کر سکتے

Ghost Love

Divine Lover

If we are children of the stars
(and all the space in between)
And our union comes together:
Spilling into infinity.

With every glance and touch
sourced from all of the unseen;
every breath and gentle kiss
a silent prayer to our dream;
do you know just how wonderful
a love like that can be?

Morning Jewel

I slip through the morning dew;
flickering cascades of glitter;
limbs dance through iridescence
as the sun bathes my skin.

It makes me smile, closed-eyed
because it warms me, delicately,
and I love falling, so much
When it's your heart I land on.

Hypnos Counts to 3

The air blinks, and we plunge into
the quietest corner of the night;
a deep dive into the temple of Hypnos
where everything multiplies by 3,
and the quiet is filled by you and me;
and the rhythm of your breath
puts a scorpid hex on my neck;
Suddenly I can't tell the difference
between you and the air I breathe.

The Lover's Prayer

Cradle me in the night-time noon,
When the moon is full and supple;
So my eyes may burrow into yours
And find its peaceful rest.

Hold me gently, then follow me home
To my garden of milk, pink silks,
So my mouth may tell you gently
How I love you, how I love you
With silent words.

How I love you, my morning star.

Letters and Leaves

In the cold and barren days,
I whisper softly, your sweet name
In hopes I'll reach you, and regain
A sombre echo of your pain.

In the warmer months renewed,
When cherry blossoms come to bloom,
I'll look for you in all the hues
Of reds, and pinks, and warmer blues.

And in the months that start to fall,
I'll close my eyes and feel you all
Around me in the crisper breeze
And read your letters in the leaves.

Rest peaceful my sweet, so you can
wake as soon as dawn breaks.

The Brightside of Blue

Black is the colour of the night time air,
white is the colour of the moon and stars,
but blue is the colour of night time's kiss;
so gently wrapped around the moon,
and over all the rustling leaves.

So gently.

A thumb brushed delicately over parted lips.

So gentle it is hard to miss,
But is so easily missed.

Gently Go Love

Quietly, go, love, there is no peace to be found in these tumultuous seas. Hold steady your compass for the old redwood trees,

And when you arrive

Lightly, go, love, and make haste with your bliss. Seal your benevolence with a solemn kiss, to the one you've quietly loved all your days, and be still in your truth, hand in hand, as we go, gently, love.

Now, gently, go, love.

Quietly

In my hands, so gently
I held you in my hands
So gently, in my hands.

In my heart, so softly
I loved you in my heart
So softly, in my heart.

In the night, so quietly
You left me in the night
So quietly in the night.

The Aftertaste

The gentle drumming of god's fingers on the tin roof made me grin about the time I knocked on your door, and you let me in;

I'll tilt my neck while I trace my fingers down the spine of the decanter, and up again, just like how you'd do it to my neck before pouring me out like that sweet ruby red, that has such delicate notes if savoured slowly behind the cage of your tongue.

But I can't ever get enough, and maybe the sore kick to the head reminds me of you; Afterall, the sour aftertaste on my stained lips go well with my morning cigarette.

The Night Knows Your Name

Sorrow

Bright Hearts

There is a glimmer of sugar-glitter reflecting
rainbows on the rim of that half empty cup,

And a baby blue moon peeks out chiefly
full on the day that your heart dies.

A trail of your favourite sweet breads leading
to the candy-skull house of the one that broke the
altar

Of the god that you fervently worship
that sits in some placid tomorrow.

That is why the wiseman never wins the trophies.

Bright hearts are always joined by sleep in a sombre
bed.

Gold Dust

The trees, sprinkled gold dust, these

leaves that kissed the other side

(that I could barely see, but felt)

of the shade I was in: I let gloom

embrace me warmly in the shade

as the leaves fell, tiling the tomb

of my heart. Sanctuary, you are wise

to give me home here, but somehow

I still crush beautiful things under;

under the soles of my feet.

Polyglot

The static is quiet enough, it feels like whispers near my hairline telling me sweet things in some foreign language I can't understand.

And I remember how the ocean kisses the sand, and I've never wanted that to stop, and I've wanted so many things to stop.

So, I keep urging my skin to crawl, but the noise isn't my friend.

It never was, but I'm not supposed to give up until I speak the language.

Secret Garden

Petals fall and line the ground

As if she cries beautiful tears, too;

This garden was always forgiving

and proud, but at night she held:

My secrets are so heavy, tucked

Into the crevasses of whites, blues,

Reds, yellows, purples, too, finding

Solace in shadows, secret rooms

With walls as high as my faith,

But if it rains, I will drown here;

I'll eventually float again, I hope

She cries, so I look up sometimes.

I never knew 'goodbye'
could also mean 'I love you'

Honey Tea in the Study

Nightly, I stood in his study in my long red dress
And the neighbours made noises I could not digest
While their honey dripped from the ceiling

and onto my neck.

I hated myself for letting love be my lover
Where the antidote to everything was to love harder
And to give up all the honey that you saved for your tea
In the conditioned conditions of unconditionally.

I let myself drown in the room that night
And in the last moments I drowned at the sight
Of moonlight, through window, glowing gold to the floor
As the room looked like the heaven that could save us.

Let's move out please

For every word that left your lips,
I'd try to breach your fingertips,
but I'd hit that bloodied brick-wall,
or fall through the floor
or the arch in your hallway
that never actually held a door.

Funeral March

An army of Sakura perform a funeral march
Down the river next to our mother's home.
The air is as fragrant and gentle as the spring,
But cold, through the piercing winter of my mother's heart;

but today is special.

On these days, the Sakura comes early, and that makes me smile.

It flushes my cheeks as my lips turn from pink, to red, to blue;

But today it's the only thing that's blue.

And I'll join the funeral march, and let the trees
bury me in pastels, as the wind sings my
mother's song, and the river rocks me to sleep.

Vampire Heart

Why do I wish to douse the light
of all the beautiful and bright,
and make all the seen, unseen
like every hidden in-between?

(masked by a flittering blink)

Maybe I've lost faith in the unknown
For every truth beautifully bold
tugged at my chains when I was sold
to all the damned and darkest souls.

(and I learned to stand on my own)

And if in part, in all my slumber
I found my heart in roaring thunder,
      will I start to fall apart
      if they daylight hits my heart?

Distortion

She wore a veil over her eyes
that made everything shine
like diamonds and silver,

but they don't colour in the lines,
and so, she'd dip in and out of
illusory sleep, or wake

(I'm not sure which)

back and forth into
dream and distortion

where things only made sense
if she didn't trust herself

Tea parties

Gauze a cuboid of my heart
And steep it in a boiling brew
Of lavender and honey milk
And serve it in a pot for two.

Take three more, and lay it on
a pile of crumbled sugar glass
that scraped the insides of me
and left me with a rotting mess:

that was my brain, but then again,
my sedation hates to smile, but
sometimes will, and sometimes I'll
sip on the tea, and smile a while.

Anguish

Bottom of the Deep

The ghosts of the greatest voyages lost at sea, found their wreckage in your swollen eyes and all I want to do is tell you how beautiful it is down deep, but they won't stop screaming.

Star Bright

I saw myself burning

bright star in the sky

    fire, fire

with tears in my eyes

and the grief that leaked

pouring over my skin

left me begging for more

left me writhing within

'til the ashes came crumbling

From my toes, to the ground

as my start came and left me

and then there was no sound.

Heart Apocalyptica

I do not fear the end of days
mountains cracked open and
it rained Hades from a molten sky
but I never feared this kind.

It was a passionate rage, singeing
blackberries on my muddy face;
and I can't help it when I smile
-do I sin when I call you mine?

I never feared the end of days
I never prayed for the world to wait
and it burns but the sound is like
you; you and I on a beautiful day
so, I burned at the edge of the lake.

Gesso

Swivel the brush in the
gesso, white on my olive
branch fell in the mud;
brown, caramel essence
in the boiler, on the stove;
skin floats on the bubbles:
it will not blend but let it
harden on me, just nice
filling my stagnancies –
enough to show people
I cannot break.

Home in the Undertow

When the moon is sweet, and I can't rest
I'll take off my dress, and step into the dark
Where the sea hits the sky birthing a monstrous black.

Fear howls like a hungry wolf, inviting me into his belly,
while he smiles at me; lovingly, begging me to lose myself,
in visceral ecstasy.

My heart pounds with the crashing of the waves pulling
me in, and my mind is so quick to drown; so, drown me
and eat me and spit me out whole.

And I go too quickly because I'm reminded of home in the
undertow, where my heaven is hell for what most people
know, so I lose myself, to gain myself, and lose myself
again.

The Unfinished Paint Job

Concrete hallways brim emptiness into the horizons and there you stand, bare knuckles to the ground at your command, as it aches too much, but not quite enough, and the life of you drips to the ground; from your wrists to your fists you look around, to the horizons that you have not yet endured, as you bow your head thinking, your heart still sinking, you haven't quite finished painting the floor.

The Catacomb is my Heart

That rope that so tightly bound us mummified
my heart, the one you dried as a preservation of
purity, you said.

But it was a dehydration, isolation, and it left
splinters in my veins.

In the silence I try to pick them out with the
same needle and thread that's supposed to put
me back together.,

Though somewhere in the space
between love and anger
It really, really hurts.

Sweet Sugar Girl

Pink icing on cupcakes, white frosted hair
Baby blue candied flowers drizzle the stairs
Pink cotton candy all tangled in vines with
Pink and red lollipops, all intertwined.
Red velvet manicures, cheeks and wet lips;
Red velvet candy canes, bruises, and slits.

It's a mess! A wet mess!
She screamed on her knees,
Banging & groping the pinks and the greens
As she vomited rose coloured sugar & peas,
& the cupcakes and icing and red jellybeans.

The dogs, they came slowly, grins baring their
teeth; they licked and they licked 'til they got to
her feet.

They licked at her feet and between her toes,
They licked all the vomit, up to her nose;
The red velvet lips, and the bruises and slits,
They licked and they licked, a bottomless pit.

'Til the sweet sugar girl stopped her crying and moaned,
"good boy, good boy," as the beasts took her nose, and
her fingers and lips, and her red velvet toes; and the red
velvet turned a dark crimson red, as the little girl smiled
as they chewed on her head;

And the sweet sugar girl stopped her moaning
and sighing, and sang softly, sweet,
"I'm dying, I'm dying."

Unlatching

The unlatching of two hearts
When you threw away the key
Asks for pulsating collisions
A smash and crash, on
Every single heartbeat.

The Red Sea

Blood in the water,

Blood on the shore,

Blood through the opal sea;

Blood through my fingers

Blood on my chest

Blood torment all over me.

Fire it burns, and the ashes, they wake

And tumble and burn on the mounds.

Warrior battle-cries: seas of regret

in the wind; merciless pain, and they scream.

Scream as their skin shreds and shreds

to their bones, and they shred as their eyes

fix on me.

Through skin and the ache,

Their bones start to break,

And I cry with the blood and the sea.

Way

Castle Hearts

For all of you with castle hearts

Fill your room with sturdy things

And welcome the ones with tired eyes

And the gentle hearts of noble kings.

To know the face of god,
look around you.

Deaf Ears

Silver sunlight fell through the rustling leaves
And my heart sat still with the dandelion seeds.

A soundless heaven to awaken my mind
As my eyes brought life to the fire alive
In all the little details that still survive.

While love fell on deaf ears
and only then could I truly listen.

Love bows her head before she listens.
Love takes her time before she speaks.

Between Love and Life

Love made Life when she let go
And Life promised to lay beside her.

They exchange sweet affections,
before eyeing the tyrant in me that so badly
needs to sleep.

Tapping the soft tuft of grass
they offer me a place in between,
and for tired hearts, that is
the warmest place to be.

I want to bring the wine
but my home is on the other
side of that river. They say they'll wait,

but can they wait long enough, when
I can never seem to keep my balance
through the house of Time.

Live as found though you'll die tomorrow
and you'll remember why you're here today.

The Choice of Death

If all of creation is divine,
Tear down your walls.

Pour your love out like a waterfall
In this unequivocal surrender
To your undying spirit.

In solitude, and abundance,
and complete absolution;

Unbeknownst as he goes, and she goes,
And their egos ricochet off the shells
Of your beautiful old fortress;

While you stay in this epiphany
Of unconditional love.

Whatever you endure,
will endure you.

Every Gardener Knows God

Peel back the layers of my chest, lover
Unpack me as the gift they say
we are: a gift unto the world.

Empty the cavity until nothing
fill me, lover, and sing softly;
tend to your garden of roses.

My love, fill me with roses,
and let the roots weave into my spine.
I'll lay out my palm for you, lover;
Let me hold one, please –

I want to know god.
I want to know what it feels
to have life in me, lover,
and death in my hand.

Living in harmony with your truth
is a choice you must keep choosing
daily.

House of Glass

If my body is a vessel, a temple made of pearls,
with no walls, or ceilings, and a bottomless ocean
for a floor; a dark Monet at the surface with
delicate glass petals from the river Styx, singing
like how you would imagine a snowflake would
sound when it forms.

And you suddenly have the ears of god,
And suddenly, the sight of god

As shadows flicker through midnight leaves and
the moon turns the pool into muted, rainbow
glitter.

Take off your shoes when you walk
through, and leave no trace.

Bathe in the pool and do not hesitate.

When it cuts through your skin,
you won't feel a thing;
pain is such a mortal sin;

Let it grace you, erase you, as you lament
within, and explode like a dying star and diffuse
into nothing, and everything:

The death of your body,
The freedom of your soul.

Maybe

I cannot pirouette there
at the edge of the world
the wind has a sharp edge
slicing me wide, open heart
the truth stung my eyes,
hope was not my friend
and life was no longer
kindness, not much of it
made me blind where it
wasn't sight, but the sound
of a deafening death of me
death in the day of maybe

Healing

Forest Magic

For magic won't go very far
sealed tightly in a mason jar
for, behold, the twinkling light
in the glow of a firefly
is not beholden to you, nor I,
nor our castles in the sky;
but still, we're just the same
in the daylight of our pain
and you are magic, in the dark,
and the firefly is in your heart.

The one who bears the weight
is the one who learns the lessons.

The River at Dawn

I hiked on a trail of boulders and bones
where the sticks cut my knees
and my tears weighed of stones.

The air through my hair kissed my cheeks
whispered clear, singing "darling, be swift,
you're not safe here."

They told me the river would lead me to you,
but the river led me to my heart renewed.

Aiora Aali

We have to get a little lost
to find the way which fits us most.

The Weaver's Hands

Each tapestry is a broken heart, laid out for the world to see. Silks and golds line the fragile parts — a complicated mastery best understood from a distance, 'til a buyer comes with gentle hands, and undo the silks and golds, and sell them to the greedy man, and be left with your vulnerable thread, and he'll smile, instead, and make a bed of roses for you to lay on.

Diora Dali

Peace is on the other side of your pain.

Cherry Blossom

Every time it rains,

Feel the earth cry

With you, my love

And when the rain stops,

Feel the earth sigh

With you, my love

Cradled by the sun,

Kissed by the moon,

Feel the earth love,

With you, my love.

Dig your toes in the sand,

With the wind on your face,

Feel the earth stand

With you, my love.

colo

My Monster Friend

I've been told that there's a monster in my brain;

they tell me if I feed him, he'll drive me insane;

but I've met my monster, and he's an honest fool:

a hard teacher, a gentle beast, and he showed me all the rules.

When the sun kisses your face, let her lay beside you and hold her dear, and listen closely as she whispers clear, "warrior child, get up and fight."

Heart Song of Love in the Grey

Look towards the sky, watch the rain fall;
She's crying for the dead of the day.
She wants just to say, join hands and pray
And be glad for the sun on its way.

Look at the birds sing through sorrow,
They don't know what comes from dismay;
There's only one thing the birds want to sing
It's the heart song of love, in the grey.

Look towards your heart my sweet lover;
There's much to be had in your pain.
Stand quietly still, hold onto your will
Let the oceans run wild through your veins.

We hear you wish upon the stars.
Know all the ancients wish upon you,
and speak in the sound of silence.

Song of The Ocean King

Let the ocean fall from your eyes,
When your heart-ship has capsized,
But wait for the rainbow in the clear,
And hold your head steady, up to the pier.

Fear not the rough and tumble, come,
For what was sung can be unsung, so
Beat your heart upon the drum, and
Drown in the tenderness of the Sun.

Breathe in the air of the wailing storm,
Battle-cry for the dead and forlorn,
And let the salt-water bathe your skin,
And sing the song of the Ocean King.

It isn't who you are in fear,
it's who you are in gladness.

Tame the Beast

One hand on your heart, then count to ten:
Here is the moment we start again,
And again, four, five, six, and the release;
Hear the chords of my breath, beneath.

Like the lullaby that once put you to sleep,
But this one's for your demons to keep
Away from the growling beast in your chest

The pulse of the wild in the night.

I'd been waiting to turn my world upside down, but I finally came to realise I'd become an expert at walking on my hands.

Andante

And when you reach the fork in the road
Remember what it is that lifts your head
Gently, when you feel the dread,
So your eyes never look upon the dirt you walk on,
but the sky and the trees that embrace you.

And though the road may be rough and torrid still,
Remember the heart you keep inside you
And your skin glittered with speckled dust,
So, you'll never forget the warmth of life,
And how your feet kiss the earth when you walk.

Before you comply with your world view,
be sure you've checked the mirror, too.

The Night King

We hear you wish upon the stars
Know all the ancients wish upon you
And speak in the sound of silence.

We will cover the earth in a blanket tonight
Of darkness and the most furious starlight
To keep you safe and close to all, and one
Universe that whispers love in your ear
And the breeze that caresses your raven hair
And the water that still cradles you to sleep.

Let your heart flood gold into the earth,
And let the noise wait outside your gates.
For tonight, you are a child of the stars,
And the ancients, and every saving grace.

Fire

Lucifera

Stag-horned crown, raven hair
Eyes that lock the deepest stare:
Lucifera has a gentle touch;
'pon a throne of bones she'll meet you.

Parted sea of crimson heads
Screaming cries from all the dead
She'll laugh at you as she softly says,
"There is no heaven here."

In roaring seas, the time then came
She told me to speak forth her name.
Her laughter shone the moon, sublime,
As she dug her nails into my spine
and welcomed me to life.

Little Icarus

Just like the air that breaks the sea,

I am weightless where my heart plays

with the breeze; trailing sweet, echoed

memory filled with laughter and tears,

sprinting spritely over water,

setting fire to my fear.

The unholy rebirth

The tears of Poseidon waged
a war, rage with the night;
supernova in the abyss —
angels, hark now hear them
break and scatter, heart pieces
sharp staccato into deep thunder
hail divinity over my people
I want to hear them howl,
growl Fenrir, and welcome
The most unholy rebirth

Part Magic

If she runs with the wolves, she's a savage
No mother's daughter, no lover's quest.
If she howls at the moon, she's barbaric,
But she's free with the wind, she is free.

If she hunts like a beast, she's a manic,
Picking apart walking corpses for meals.
They don't really know she's part magic
Toothpicks and bones, she's a witch.

Sing to the moon of your tales of the past.
Jump off a cliff to the sea, make a splash.
Don't dive too deep, for you'll drown,
Oh, you'll drown, but stay long enough

To make breath like a vow; and a promise
To you and your own that you'll keep
Howling and running, singing and jumping
'til the moon burns and the sun sleeps.

Garden Girl

The girl is chained because she is wild.

The beast in her belly is a garden of wildflowers waiting to be birthed from her mound; ready to violate, desiccate, every impermeable dead thing-King with a pulse.

And she'll look at him while she fists blood into the carvings of the palace walls, convulsing in the wicked ecstasy he brought her to for his midnight meal.

Every night, she'll love him with all of the flowers that come, and come, and come again.

When We Spill

Outline the shape of him,
Silver light, drunken eyes;
The silhouette of my heart
I do yearn for his warmth.

My angel wields a sword
piercing through the skin of me
deep into the midnight zone
where hell is just a tea party.

Depth is heavy, but how I love
to break, and how I love to lose,
my mind to him: holy when we

hollow: holier when we fill;
holy in the gracious night
and we spill, and we spill

Holy Water

Bathe me in creamy decadence, so sweet and thick, and I will let you bring your best cards, so grace can swallow us whole.

Like a savage she'll swallow us whole.

And envelope us in transcendental bliss, when she binds our eyes, transfixed; in brutal fire and desperate thirst to be quenched by the mutuality of our nakedness: naked eyes, mind, and as one throbbing heart, we rest,

As we are reborn in holy water, by every burning sun.

Mango Salad

I will let the mangoes flood your garden at night
And when you wake, I'll show you the sweetest sin:
A red sea of sweet-meats glow under a furious
sun.

It seeps between our toes, pressed against our
soles, and I'm not sorry about all the battles we
lost.

The crows have come to share, a symphony
laughing at the wicked mess, so loud, it sounds like
we finally made hell scream.

And we'll let the sugar water flood our feet;
I'll arch my back as it consumes me,
Groping the bones at either side..

And I'll call you close, so you can take your
indulgent place beside me and make a meal of me,
sweet nectar of my honeyed heart.

Throne Room

If I comb my fingers through the leaves
Will I meet your crimson bloom?

Through the hollows of your ebony pearls
I'll learn my darkest truths; and I'll look
Into those soul-filled eyes and start
Howling at the moon.

If I trail my fingers down your spine,
And kiss you at each rise and fall,
Will I hear the ocean or the evergreens?
Or the whisper of the ancients' crawl?

I'll smoke you like the summer breeze
And leave my trail down to your ruins

And pour new life into your cup
And make a throne room of your womb.

Kali

The sun peeked over the horizon
And my heart thumped a steady beat.
A fearsome woman stood before me:
Wild hair, wide eyed, bare breasted,
Skin like coal, tongue like fire
Outstretched arms, swinging hips;

Closer, closer, slow, velvet steps.
Head jerking side-to-side, side-to-side
Teeth bared in an inexhaustible grin
"Hello, child," she whispered, grim.
"I'm here to see your truth."

Ancestral Ride

If winged beasts take us to the mountain tops in marble caves that stand alone, let the most vicious ones take us for a hell ride to our posts, where we can wave our silver flags alone, and together in a unison of knowing

Beat the skinned drum of the ancients with soiled bone, as the sun rises and sets, as an offering to our ancestors: alive as the oceans rage against the tides, as the thunder roars in the storms, amongst our trees that sigh a giant breath, lungs of the earth.

Love is in ruin.

While our people meddle, with heads glued to the ground, as we breathe into the sky, and gently whisper prayers into the wind.

Home

the Cracks

Between the cracks, I felt
spaces to breathe, between
the fortress of you, ancient.
Beloved, you told me I was
(silently, beautifully, hidden)
and so somehow it felt kind
to put my fingers there.

In All the Ways

In all the ways I have known you
I love to know you in-between
the folds of your breath, against me
as how the ocean loves the shore.

So, cradle me in the warmth of you;
a gentle current on a silent night
I will not hold you tight, but I will
be here in our calmer tide, as this

Day lays to rest, and my breath
falls on your chest – rise and fall
into the softest place: this heart
I have known in all the ways.

When the golden hour come,
flowers bloom towards the sun.

On Love

Love is not the embellishment
of diamonds on withered soul

Nor is it the bath of rose petals
you wash your grime in
from hard existence.

It is the bread and butter of life
for which you receive as holy
communion, giving from yourself
as you honour the Divine.

Love is found
in the gentle push
and pull between
the screaming yeses
and hard nos.

Whispering Stars

Lay with me under the big oak tree,
And let's rename the stars;
listen to the soft murmurings
Of the moon from afar.

And wait until the daffodils
Lay sunshine on the fields;
'Til the morning dew passes through
Melting off the lemon peels.

'Til the horizon blinks wide open, inviting
Children like scattered glitter, delighting
In the last thing they ate
And the first thing they saw
And the ways in which they learn.

Lay with me under the big oak tree,
And let's rename our hearts.

And every night before you lay your head,
make an altar of your bed.

I'm listening

They say timing is everything
But in my joy, I interrupt, abrupt,
and you'll tell me to follow through;

So, with my words and hands, I do.
In my embarrassment, I'll squeeze you
And listen to every tongue and click
Of your tongue and lips;

Tongue and lips, I want to kiss.
I smile because you keep me so warm,
but nothing is funny, and I'm listening.

Shade of the Palm

Rustling leaves through opaque curtains.
And the sun kisses our faces, gibberish.
She wants to play, but I melt into you
And tell her *later*.

I let your breath warm me
Rise and fall, rise and fall;
High tide, cover my eyes
With the shade of your palm.

I know why the bluebird sings

Baby, I know why the bluebird sings.

Like the higher octaves of a baby grand
She sang with no particular song at hand.

Like scattered raindrops in major key
The soundtrack to our opening scene

Where the bluebirds play
By our window pane

With our kisses as good mornings,
Every good morning

And the baritone of your breath as you wake.

Baby, I know why the bluebird sings.

Cherry Braille

I'll draw the honey from your lips
And paint it down the shadow from
Your chin towards the subtle ridge
Where your breath is hard to swallow.

I'll trace the finger up the trail
With the sharpness of my nail
And leave small drops of dessert rain
Planting cherry seeds in written braille.

More than
happiness
you deserve
magic.

The Night Knows Your Name

About the author

Born to a household of conservative Filipino values, Dvora found it hard to find a place in the world. Although never having lived in the Philippines, she was torn between living with the Australian norms of her friends, and appeasing her conservative parents.

This displacement fuelled much of the friction in her life which contributed to the mental health issues she suffered. As a result, she has sought to find herself, and figure out why she couldn't manage life without a constant battle, which fed into her love and passions in philosophy, spirituality, and psychology. Although seemingly helpful for phases at a time, nothing worked long enough. She was only to be diagnosed bipolar II, CPTSD, and social anxiety when she was 30..

This diagnosis cracked the hardened shell that softened her voice, and she began to write, sketch, and compose music as she always wanted to when she was a little girl. Through her creations, Dvora now aims to spread love, and inspire hope for those who struggle with mental illness, fostering acceptance of the human condition in a society that presents a standard of perfection as the norm. There is no light without dark. There is no joy without sorrow.

We are human, and the whole of us is beautiful.

The Night Knows Your Name

dvora dali

www dvoradali.com
@ @dvoradali
✉ lovedvoradali@gmail
f /lovedvoradali

www.ingramcontent.com/pod-product-compliance
Lightning Source LLC
Chambersburg PA
CBHW021132020426
42331CB00005B/738